Happy Endings

FINISHING THE EDGES OF YOUR QUILT

Mimi Dietrich

Dedication

With Love to my Family

Acknowledgements

Many, many thanks to

My Mom and Dad, who taught me to finish things.

Bob, Jon, and Ryan Dietrich for teaching me the value of the computer and giving me time to use it.

Laurie Scott for her professional consultations and support.

Kathy Cook for her encouragement and experience.

John Haw for his journal entry.

Norma Campbell, Dallas Clautice, Sheila Rousseaux, and Jackie Schlesinger for their contributions.

Dottie Hunt for help in finishing many of the samples.

Nancy Martin and her staff for giving my dream a happy ending.

Credits

Photography . . . . Carl Murray
Illustration and Graphics . . . . Stephanie Benson

Happy Endings—
Finishing The Edges Of Your Quilt©
© Mimi Dietrich, 1987

Printed in the United States of America
03 02   27

Library of Congress Card Number 87-051214
ISBN: 0-943574-44-7

Contents

She remembered the phone call. She had just finished the quilt. I called then, she told me she was done, but there was an edge to her voice. She felt funny about it, couldn't explain the feeling.

"You feel sad," I said.

She remembered that. How did I know?

The fun in creating it, the joy in doing it, that was gone with the quilt finished. It was true. She did feel sad.

A friend once called her a process person. Quilters and writers use the same language. We both like holding the finished product in our hands, but the important thing is the process. We want to stay in it as long as we can and do it as well as we can.

Ending a quilt is a process. There's a joy in the doing. So if it must end, let it be a happy ending.

A Writer's Journal
John Haw, April 1987

Choosing a Happy Ending For Your Quilt

As quilters we love to choose fabric colors, textures, and prints to create new designs for our quilts. We find a wonderful peace in quilting the layers of soft fabric. But many of us hastily complete the last step of the quiltmaking process — finishing the edges. Many books, magazines, and patterns simply say, "Bind the quilt edges". **Happy Endings** gives you choices and directions so that this stage of making your quilt can also be creative.

As you plan your quilt, consider the technique that will frame your design. There are many methods for finishing the edges of your quilted project, encasing the batting and cut edges of the front and back of the quilt. The style of your quilt may determine the appearance of your final border. The quilt's purpose may determine the durability of your finishing method. Your time and available fabric may also be a factor as you complete your quilt. If you are planning to enter your quilt in a show, you will be looking for the perfect Happy Ending. Reading through this chapter will help you make an appropriate choice for the finishing touch on your special quilt.

Some quilts can be completed without a binding. Very often comforters are finished by placing the front and back of the quilt right sides together on the batting and sewing around the edge, then turning the quilt right side out. The edges usually have a puffy look and this technique works best when the quilt is tied or scantily quilted. A row of hand or machine quilting near the edge can give the illusion of binding. A similar method can be used after the quilting is completed, turning under the front and back of the quilt and stitching the edges together by hand. These techniques are used when you do not want a row of binding along the edge of the quilt, or possibly because you do not have a binding to match.

Using the backing fabric of your quilt to create binding is an easy, quick, and inexpensive way to complete your quilt. All it requires is an extra inch of backing fabric extending beyond the front of the quilt in all four directions. This inch is turned over the cut edges of the front to cover the batting and finish the edges. With this method the corners can be quickly overlapped or mitered for a finer appearance. If the backing fabric does not coordinate with the front, this method can also be done in reverse — turning the front of the quilt to the back. This is a fast way to finish your quilt using either hand or machine stitching.

For a more professional finish, you can make your own binding. It requires extra fabric to make the binding, so you need to plan ahead and save fabric for this last step. Your own binding can complement your design by framing the edge of the quilt or matching the background fabric in the design. It can accent a solid border with print binding or simply create a perfect match to your favorite fabric in the quilt. A straight or diagonal design in a fabric can be used to create a special binding. Little flowers or hearts printed in a row on your fabric can be cut to line up along the edges of your binding. Striped fabric can be cut so that a single stripe accents your design or so that the stripes spiral around the edge of your quilt. Patches of several fabrics can be pieced together to create a rainbow binding. Unique finishing touches are possible when you make your own binding.

Binding can be made using the straight grain of your fabric, cut parallel to the woven threads. Straight binding has very little stretch and should be used for straight edges and square corners. To provide stretch to ease around curves, binding should be made using the bias or diagonal grain of the fabric. To make a strip of binding long enough to complete your quilt, strips can be pieced together or cut as one continuous strip.

Binding can be applied using various techniques. Traditional binding covers your quilt edges with a single layer of fabric,while the French method adds a more durable double layer of binding. If your quilt has large solid areas of color in the corners or wide outer borders, very often you can round off the corners of your quilt. This makes it easy and quick to sew the binding to the edges. If your quilt has small squares in the corner design of the border or has a design that requires a perfectly square corner, you can miter the four corners of the quilt or easily fold the fabric to create the miters. Binding can also be applied to scalloped edges. For a special effect, you may want to insert cording between the binding and the quilt.

If you are a creative quilter, try a special finishing technique for the edge of your quilt. For a very special quilt, you can use prairie points. It requires extra fabric to make the points, but they create a very unique border for your design. It's a fun way to match colors from the design or repeat a triangular pattern from the quilt.

A baby quilt or a feminine design may lend itself to a ruffled edge. This also requires extra fabric, so plan ahead. You can repeat a favorite fabric in the ruffle or use pre-gathered eyelet lace or gathered trim for a fun and frivolous edge. Instead of gathering a ruffle, the same strip of fabric can be pleated for an unusual quilt edge.

Cording can be covered with fabric and inserted between the front and back of the quilt. This creates a coordinating accent to complement one of the colors in your quilt.

Many of the techniques included in this book can be applied to other quilted projects. Clothing such as vests or jackets often require binding or finished edges. Totebags and other items for the home may benefit from these ideas.

Quilted projects may be completed using either hand or machine stitches. A Stitching Guide, found on page 46, has been included to provide specific directions for the stitches used to add a finishing touch to your quilt.

Whether you choose a quick front-to-back finish, use the back of the quilt to bind your edges, make your own binding, or add special effects, may you discover a Happy Ending for your quilting project.

Finishing Your Quilt Without Binding

Some quilts are finished without binding. The front and back of the quilt are simply sewn together by hand or machine to enclose the batting. This technique is used when you do not want a row of binding on the edge. It's a good technique to use when you do not have binding fabric to match your quilt.

Hand Finishing

If the quilting is already completed on your quilt, you should use a hand sewing method to sew the front and back of the quilt together. As you quilt, it is important to stop your quilting stitches 1/2" from the quilt edge to allow space for the finishing seam. Trim the front and back of the quilt so that the cut edges are 1/4" larger than the finished size of the quilt. Trim the batting 1/8" smaller than the finished size of the quilt. Fold the front of the quilt over the batting, turning under the 1/4" seam (Figure 1). Turn the back of the quilt under 1/4" and pin the folded edge to match the front of the quilt (Figure 2). Stitch the edges together using the slipstitch, sewing the front and back folds together to complete your quilt (Figure 3).

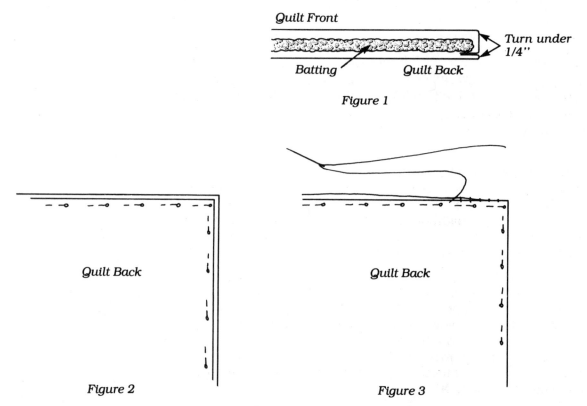

Quilt Front

Turn under 1/4"

Batting   Quilt Back

Figure 1

Quilt Back

Figure 2

Quilt Back

Figure 3

Machine Finishing

If you want to sew the edges together by machine, this should be done before the actual quilting process. This method works best when you are planning to tie your quilt or quilt it for a puffy effect. It is difficult to closely quilt a large area after the edges have been stitched. This is a good method to use for a child's fluffy quilt or for a comforter.

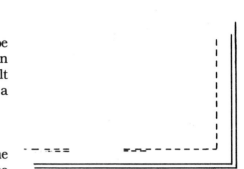

Quilt Front and Back

Figure 4

First place the front and back of the quilt right sides together. Pin the edges and trim the front and back even. Sew a 1/4" seam around the four sides of the quilt. This stitching will keep the front and back of the quilt together as you attach the batting. Backtack, leaving an opening on one side, not too close to a corner (Figure 4). For a small quilt, the opening should be 6 to 10 inches; for a large quilt it may need to be as large as 20 inches.

Lay the batting out smoothly on a flat surface and pin the quilt to the batting, placing the front of the quilt down next to the batting. Pin around all of the edges of the quilt and batting, letting the fuzzy batting edges extend beyond the quilt. They will be trimmed later. Sew the quilt to the batting, following the 1/4" seam allowance on the back and leaving the same opening as before (Figure 5). Now trim the batting close to the stitching, making sure you do not cut your fabric. To turn the quilt right side out, reach through the opening between the front and back of the quilt. Pull the corners through the opening, one corner at a time, and turn the quilt right side out. As you turn each corner, fold the two seam allowances over the batting before you pull it out (Figure 6). This will create pointed corners when it is turned right side out.

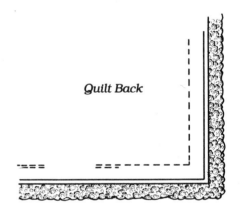

Quilt Back

Figure 5

The opening is stitched closed by first trimming the batting to the finished size of the quilt. Fold the front seam allowance over the batting. Turn the quilt backing under 1/4" and pin it to the front. Stitch the opening together using the slipstitch (Figure 7).

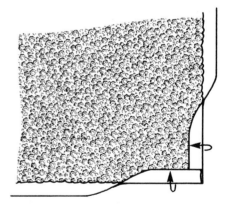

Figure 6

Before quilting, a small quilt can be straightened out on a tabletop, but a large quilt may require a large floor area and a friend. Tug on opposite sides of the quilt to straighten the three layers of the quilt so that the front, back, and batting lie smoothly. Baste or pin the three layers together before quilting or tying your quilt.

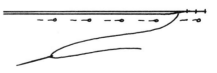

Figure 7

Rounded Corners

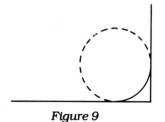

Figure 8

Before sewing the front and back together, the corners of your comforter or quilt may be softened by rounding off the square corners. If there are wide borders on your quilt, or wide areas of background fabric in the corners of your design, you can round off the corners. If there is a definite square pattern in the corners, it will look better if you keep the corners square.

Figure 9

Rounded corners can easily be made using a round dish. Use a cup for a slightly rounded corner, a saucer for a more rounded curve, or a dinner plate for a large quilt. Position the plate in one corner so that the circle touches both sides of the quilt (Figure 8). Using a pencil, draw along the curve from side to side, creating a perfectly rounded corner (Figure 9). Cut along the line and repeat this on all corners on the front and back of your quilt (Figure 10).

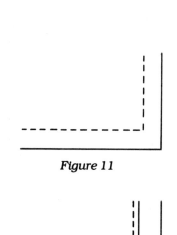

Figure 10

Sew the front and back of the quilt together as before, being careful not to stretch your fabric as you sew around the curves.

Imitation Binding

After you have stitched the front and the back of the quilt together and have turned it right side out, you can create the look of binding along the edge. Sew a row of hand or machine quilting 1/4" to 1/2" from the edge seam (Figure 11). This row of quilting makes a ridge along the edge that gives the illusion of binding. It also flattens down the puffy edge. This looks especially nice when the back of the quilt matches the border fabric on the front.

Figure 11

To give the appearance of wide binding, plan to stitch a 1"-2" wide border on your quilt before you finish the edges. Sew the front and the back of the quilt together by hand or machine, then quilt along the last border seam (Figure 12). This last border will appear to be wide binding.

Figure 12

Appliqued Border

To create a very unusual finishing touch, applique a curved or scalloped border to the edge of your quilt front. Your border will have the soft look of scallops without binding the curved edges. Sew the front and the back of the quilt together along the straight edges and quilt along the applique curves for a very special quilt finish (Figure 13).

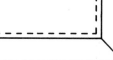

Figure 13

Finishing Your Quilt With Backing

Some quilts appear to have binding along the edges but are actually finished without making a separate binding. By turning the backing fabric over the batting and front edge of the quilt, you can easily and quickly complete your project.

This technique requires the back of the quilt to be cut larger than the front of the quilt. Very often in planning a quilt, the backing fabric is already longer and wider than the front. This method economically uses up that extra fabric. It's an appropriate method to use if you do not have extra fabric to make binding. Make sure that your backing fabric coordinates with the quilt design. If not, you may want to reverse the process, turning the quilt front fabric to the back to create the finished edge.

After quilting your project, trim the batting even with the front cut edge of the quilt, being careful not to clip through the back of the quilt. Lay the quilt on a flat surface and sew a basting stitch around all four edges of the quilt. Baste 1/4" from the cut edge of the quilt top, stitching through the quilt front, batting, and backing (Figure 1). This step will keep the 3 layers from shifting as you complete the edges.

For 1/2" wide "binding" you will need one inch of backing fabric extending beyond the front of the quilt. Use a clear ruler to measure one inch of extra fabric around all edges of the quilt, then trim the backing carefully (Figure 2). For binding wider than 1/2", cut the extending fabric two times the desired binding width.

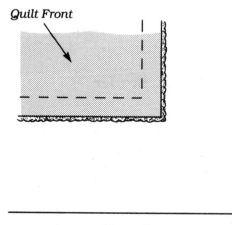

Figure 1

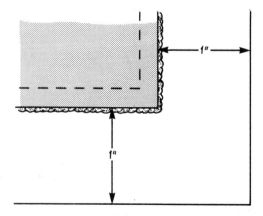

Figure 2

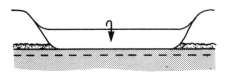

Figure 3

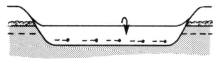

Figure 4

Straight Edges

Fold the backing fabric in half, wrong sides together, so that the cut edge of the back meets the cut edge of the front (Figure 3). Fold again along the front edge of the quilt to form the finished edge (Figure 4). This encases the batting and covers 1/2" of the front edge. Pin along the first fold to hold the finished edge in place.

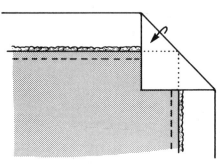

Figure 5

Figure 6

Overlapped Corners

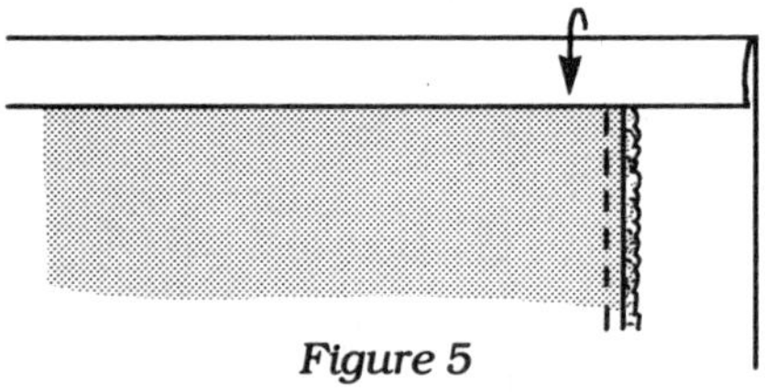

The four corners can be finished using two methods. The quickest method is to continue folding the corners as you fold the sides. Fold the first side, extending the folds to the corners (Figure 5). Then fold the second side, overlapping the first (Figure 6). This is the fastest method, however it can be bulky and threads of fabric sometimes sneak out of the corner fold. It helps to sew the corners closed by hand.

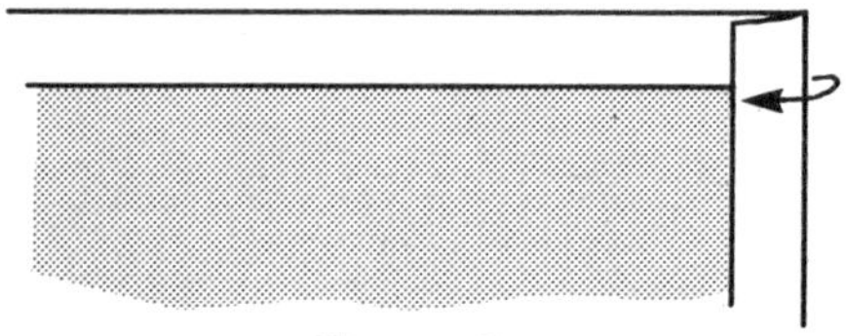

Mitered Corners

To improve the corner appearances, you can fold a miter. It only takes a few minutes longer — and remember there are only four corners on your quilt! In this method, the corners are folded first, then the sides.

First fold the corner of the quilt backing over the point of the quilt front (Figure 7). The fold touches the corner point of the front. Then fold the sides, so that the edge of the back meets the edge of the front as before (Figure 8). Fold once more to create the binding and a miter at the corner (Figure 9). Trim out the small square that extends onto the quilt and pin the folds securely before sewing (Figure 10).

Figure 7

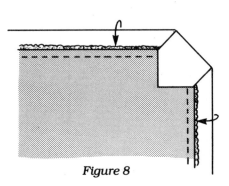

Figure 8

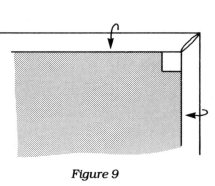

Figure 9

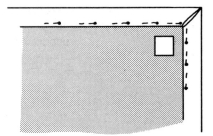

Figure 10

Hand Finishing

This "binding" can be stitched by hand or by machine. To sew by hand, start with an 18" length of thread that matches the backing fabric. Sew the binding to the front of the quilt using the blindstitch or slipstitch (Figure 11). The stitches should not go all the way through to the back of the quilt. At each mitered corner, sew up the miter with four or five blindstitches, then continue to sew the next side of the quilt (Figure 12).

After the binding has been stitched, quilt one row of stitches right next to the row of binding stitches, sewing through all three layers of your quilt (Figure 13). This quilting line will secure the edges and give the illusion of binding on the back of the quilt. Don't forget to remove your basting stitches.

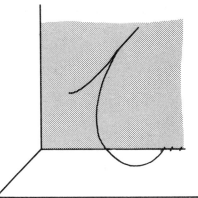

Figure 11

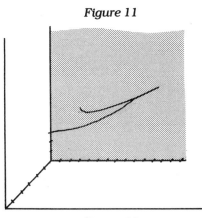

Figure 12

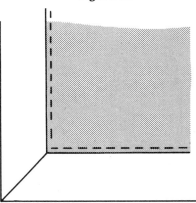

Figure 13

Machine Finishing

To finish sewing the edge by machine, simply sew around the edges of the quilt on the fold where the pins are placed (Figure 14). This sews through all layers of the quilt so it is not necessary to add the last row of quilting stitches. The corner miters can be closed with a few small blindstitches.

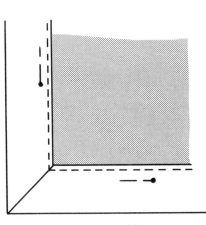

Figure 14

Finishing Your Quilt With Binding

Basting

After all of the quilting is completed on your quilt, it helps to take a little time to prepare your quilt for the binding. It is very important to baste the edges together. This is done so that the quilt front, the batting, and the quilt back become one unit. It is much easier to sew the binding to one quilt rather than three layers.

Lay your quilt on a flat surface and smooth out the front, batting, and back. The front should be on top. Pin the layers together around the edges. Baste the edges by hand 1/4" from the cut edge of the front, stitching all around the quilt. This can also be done by machine, but you need to be careful that the layers don't shift. An even-feed foot on your sewing machine will help to keep the layers together as you baste by machine.

Check the opposite sides of your quilt to make sure they are even. You can adjust the length of the quilt edges by tightening or loosening the basting stitches.

After the basting is completed, trim the batting and the back so that they are even with the front edge of the quilt. This can be done quickly with a rotary cutter. Also trim any threads that may be hanging from the front edge of the quilt. This creates a nice clean edge on your quilt so that you are ready to apply the binding.

Making Binding

It is fun and creative to make your own binding. You can use packaged binding, but binding made from your own fabric is a perfect match to the quality fabric in your quilt. It gives a coordinated look to your project, and adds a special touch. It is usually more durable than commercially made binding, and doesn't take too long to make. You will need to purchase extra fabric to frame your quilt perfectly.

Always prewash your fabric when you are making your own binding. This prevents shrinking and puckering after it is applied to your quilt.

If you do not plan to use your binding immediately after you make it, store it by winding it carefully around a paper tube. Wind it flat, not folded, and try not to stretch it.

Determining Binding Size

The length of your cut binding is determined by the distance around your quilt. Add 9" to this measurement to allow for turning corners and the finishing seam. If your quilt has scalloped edges, you need to measure around the curved edges.

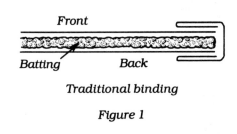

Traditional binding

Figure 1

In this book, directions for marking, cutting, and sewing binding are given for binding that is cut 2" wide. This size makes traditional binding that is finished 1/2" wide or French binding that is finished 3/8" wide. This measurement is easy to mark and cut using a 2" wide clear plastic quilter's ruler. This size binding is easy to handle as you apply it to the quilt and turn it to cover the edges.

Some quilters prefer wider bindings. You might like a wider frame for your design, or you may feel more comfortable applying a wider strip. Fabric strips can be cut wider to create wider binding, just remember to account for seam allowances, binding width on the front and back of your quilt, and the thickness of the quilt.

French binding

Figure 2

When determining the width of the binding, first consider the method that you will use to apply it. Traditional binding covers the edge with a single layer of fabric, finished approximately 1/4 of the cut size (Figure 1). Traditional binding cut 2" wide allows for two 1/2" seam allowances, 1/2" showing on the front of the quilt, and 1/2" showing on the back. If it is cut 2-1/2" wide, you will have a finished size of 5/8". If it is cut 3" wide, the finished size will be 3/4". The seam allowances change with the width of the binding. If you are using thick batting, add 1/4" to the cut size to allow the binding to turn over the thickness of the batting.

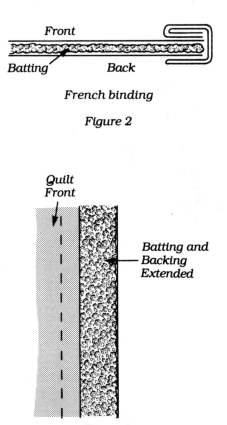

Figure 3

French binding applies a double layer of fabric, finished approximately 1/6 of the cut size (Figure 2). French binding cut 2" wide allows for two 1/4" seam allowances, 3/8" showing on the front and back of the quilt, and 3/8" for the front and back of the quilt on the inside layer. If it is cut 3" wide, the finished size will be 1/2", using 1/2" seam allowances. If you are using thick batting, add 1/4" to the cut size to allow for the batting thickness.

For both methods it is important to prepare your quilt so that the batting extends to the edge of the binding to evenly pad the binding and give it body along the edge. If your quilt design allows a 1/4" seam and you want wider bindings, you may have a small seam allowance on the front of the quilt, but let the batting and backing extend to the width of the finished binding (Figure 3).

Determining Fabric Needed

Using A Rectangle

After you have measured the distance around your quilt and determined the width of your cut binding, you can calculate the amount of extra fabric you will need to cut a separate binding.

A rectangle of fabric can be used to easily cut binding strips along the straight grain of the fabric, or to cut continuous straight or off grain binding. A rectangle can also be used to cut true bias strips and continuous cut bias binding for larger quilts.

To determine the amount of fabric you will need, divide the length of binding you need by the width of your fabric. (If you are planning to piece your strips together, subtract three inches from the width of your fabric to allow for diagonal seams.) Round off the answer to the next highest number. This will tell you how many strips you will need to cut across the rectangle. Multiply the number of strips by the width of the strips to determine how many inches of fabric you will need to cut enough binding. If you don't want to figure it out, this chart gives you the length of fabric you need if you have 40" wide fabric (45" wide fabric minus shrinkage and 3" for seam allowances).

(These quilt sizes are based on standard mattress sizes, adding 12" to the sides, top, and bottom for the quilt size.) If you are making a baby quilt with 2" wide cut binding, you will need 12" of 45" fabric to cut enough binding.

Example:
Baby Quilt with 2" binding
Length of binding ÷ width of fabric
$$219 ÷ 40 = 5.4$$
Round off 5.4 to 6 strips
6 strips × 2" width = 12" fabric needed

Standard Quilt	Size	Amount of Binding (length plus 9")	45" Fabric Length for Binding Width		
			2"	2-1/2"	3"
Baby	45" x 60"	219"	12"	15"	18"
Twin	63" x 99"	333"	18"	22-1/2"	27"
Double	78" x 99"	363"	20"	25"	30"
Queen	84" x 104"	385"	20"	25"	30"
King	100" x 104"	417"	22"	27-1/2"	33"

Using a Square

Binding strips and continuous cut binding may also be cut from a square. To determine the size of the square needed, first multiply the width of your cut binding times the length (in inches) needed for your quilt. This gives you the total number of square inches of binding, or the area of fabric needed to make your binding. Take the area of fabric needed and find its square root. (Don't faint — just get out a small calculator, enter the number, and press the square root button for the answer!) Round off this number to the next highest even number to allow extra for seam allowances. This number is the size of the square you will need to cut enough binding. If you don't want to figure it out, this chart will help.

(These quilt sizes are based on standard mattress sizes, adding 12" to the sides, top, and bottom for the quilt size.) If you are making a baby quilt with 2" wide cut binding, you will need a 22" square of fabric to cut enough binding.

Example:
Baby Quilt with 2" binding
Cut binding width x length
$$2'' \times 219'' = 438''$$
438" = area of fabric needed
$$\sqrt{438} = 22'' \text{ square}$$

Standard Quilt	Size	Amount of Binding (length plus 9")	Square for Binding Width 2"	2-1/2"	3"
Baby	45" x 60"	219"	22"	24"	26"
Twin	63" x 99"	333"	26"	30"	32"
Double	78" x 99"	363"	28"	32"	36"
Queen	84" x 104"	385"	30"	34"	36"
King	100" x 104"	417"	32"	36"	38"

Straight Grain Binding

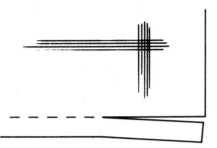

Figure 4

When you finish your quilt without binding or use the back of your quilt to finish the edges, your quilt is naturally finished with fabric that is cut on the straight grain. The threads in your fabric run parallel to the edges of your quilt.

If you wish to cut a separate binding for your quilt, it can also be cut on the straight grain (Figure 4). Simply cut strips straight across the width or length of your fabric, then sew them together to make a strip long enough to bind the edges of your quilt. You can also cut straight grain binding with the continuous cut method described later in this chapter. Straight grain binding is quick and easy to cut. It can be used on straight edges and square corners, but bias binding should be used for curves.

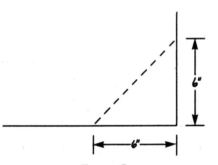

Figure 5

Bias Binding

Bias binding cut on the diagonal grain of the fabric may take a little longer to make, but it has some definite advantages. Bias binding cut on the true bias grain contains a built-in stretch that helps your binding to lie smoothly, turn curves easily, and miter corners nicely. When applied to the edge of your quilt, the bias threads crisscross the edge creating a durable finish. Binding cut on the straight grain will have one thread running along the folded edge that can weaken with wear. Bias binding can be made by cutting separate diagonal strips of fabric, or by using the continuous cut method later in this chapter.

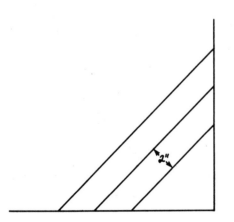

Figure 6

To cut a bias strip on the true bias grain of your fabric, start in a corner next to a selvage edge if possible. Using a ruler, make a mark 6" from the corner on each side. Connect these marks to draw a diagonal line (Figure 5). Draw a parallel line 2" away to make your first bias strip. Continue drawing parallel lines until you have enough binding strips to go around the edges of your quilt (Figure 6). Sew the bias strips together.

Sewing Binding Strips Together

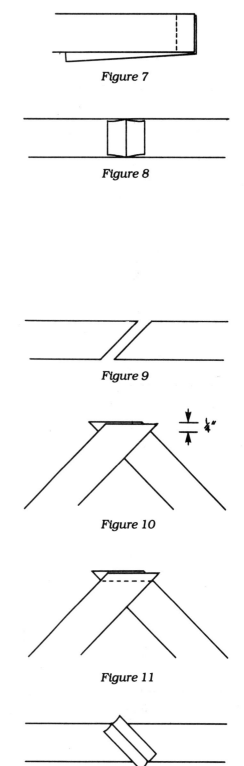

Figure 7

Figure 8

Binding can be made from strips of fabric pieced together to create one long strip. Fabric strips can be cut on the straight or bias grain of the fabric. The strip widths will all be the same, but the length of each strip will probably vary according to the fabric you are using. You may want to cut strips according to a design printed on the fabric, cut straight grain strips to conserve fabric, or cut bias strips that are different lengths. The total length of the strips should be longer than the distance around your quilt to allow for seam allowances.

The easiest way to sew the strips together is to connect the pieces using straight seams. This method, however, creates bulky areas when folded and stitched as binding. The seam overlaps itself and creates a thickness of many layers that is difficult to sew, especially on small projects. However, you may need to do this to conserve fabric. Simply place right sides together and sew a 1/4" seam using small stitches (Figure 7). Press the seam open to distribute the fullness of the seam (Figure 8).

Figure 9

Diagonal seams in your binding will improve the finished look of your project. The diagonal seam distributes the thickness of the seam when it is applied as binding. On bias binding it also follows the grain of the fabric and prevents stretching on the seam.

Figure 10

One method of attaching the strips is to cut the two strips diagonally so that they fit together. With right sides up, cut the left piece diagonally as shown and the right piece as shown so that they fit together like two puzzle pieces (Figure 9). Place the two cut edges with right sides together, matching the cut diagonal edges. Slide them so that the ends extend slightly. They should cross 1/4" from the cut edge (Figure 10). Sew a 1/4" seam by hand or machine across the cut edges (Figure 11). Open the strips to create a continuous strip of binding. Press the seam open (Figure 12). Repeat this method adding more strips of binding until you have a piece long enough to go around your quilt.

Figure 11

Figure 12

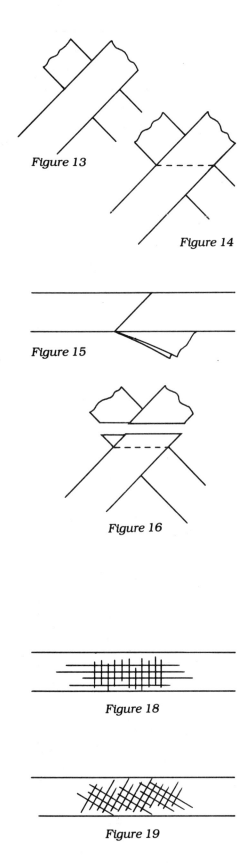

Figure 13

Figure 14

Figure 15

Figure 16

Once you have tried the previous method of attaching strips, you may want to try another. This method is fun to use as you first sew the strips quickly and accurately, then cut the seam allowances.

Before making any diagonal cuts, place your two strips right sides together, crossing the ends at right angles (Figure 13). Lay this on a flat surface and imagine the strips as a giant letter "A". Draw a line across the crossed pieces to "cross the A", then sew along the line (Figure 14). Your seam will be exact and you can unfold a continuous strip (Figure 15). You only need to trim the excess fabric off, leaving a 1/4" seam (Figure 16). Press this seam open and continue adding strips until you have enough binding (Figure 17).

Figure 17

Continuous Cut Binding

The method of continuous cut binding allows you to start with a large piece of fabric, sew one or two seams, and cut one long continuous piece of binding. It eliminates the process of sewing many separate strips together. You can cut straight grain binding, off grain binding (has a little stretch, but is not cut on the true bias grain), or true bias binding.

Figure 18

Straight grain binding (Figure 18) should only be used to bind straight edges and square corners. It has very little stretch and will not lie flat around curves and rounded corners.

Off grain binding (Figure 19) has more stretch and should be used on straight edges and moderately curved corners, but must be applied carefully so that it does not pucker.

Figure 19

True bias binding (Figure 20) is cut on the true diagonal grain of the fabric and has the best stretch. It is great to sew on any edge, straight or curved.

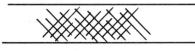

Figure 20

20

Straight Grain Continuous Cut Binding

This is the easiest binding to make, using only one straight seam. The binding is cut on the straight grain of the fabric and therefore should only be used to bind straight edges or sharp corners.

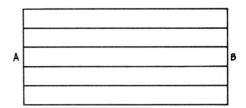

Figure 21

First determine the size of the square or rectangle that will make enough binding. Lay your fabric on a flat surface, right side up. Mark lines two inches apart parallel to one long side (Figure 21). Trim off extra fabric at the bottom (you should not have to trim if the measurement of the fabric can be divided by your binding width.)

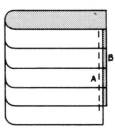

Figure 22

To make the seam, bring side A and side B together, right sides together. Shift side A down so that the top cut edge of A matches up with the first line marked on side B. At the other end of the seam, the bottom end of B should match the last line on side A (Figure 22). Sew this seam with a 1/4" seam allowance and 12-15 stitches per inch. Press this seam open.

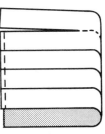

Figure 23

Using sharp scissors, start at one uneven end and cut along the marked line (Figure 23). When you get to the seam, you will have moved down one line and can continue to cut one piece of binding long enough to bind your quilt.

Off Grain Continuous Cut Binding

This binding is made like the straight binding above, except that the fabric is cut slightly off grain to give it a small amount of stretch. It can be used to bind straight edges and curves that are not too sharp. This is bias binding, but not cut on the true bias grain. The seams are stitched on a slight diagonal to distribute the thickness of the seam.

Figure 24

Determine the size of the square or rectangle that is needed to cut enough binding for your quilt. Add two inches (or the width of your binding) to this measurement. Lay your fabric on a flat surface right side up. Along sides A and B place a mark every two inches (the binding width). Draw a line from the top edge on A to the first mark on B. Continue drawing parallel lines until you reach the bottom of the fabric (Figure 24). Cut off the top and bottom triangles (Figure 25). Bring sides A and B together to sew the seam, matching the top of B to the first line on A (Figure 26). Press the seam open. Start cutting along the marked line at one uneven end to cut a continuous strip of binding.

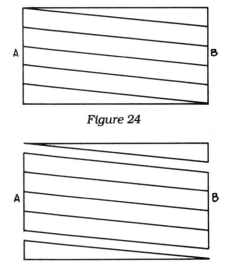

Figure 25

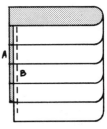

Figure 26

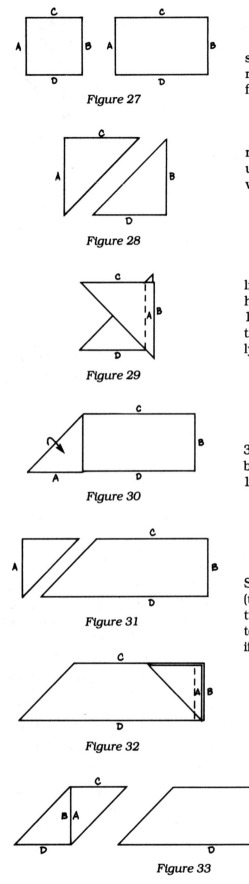

Bias Continuous Cut Binding

This method makes bias binding that will work well in any finishing situation. True bias has a stretch that allows it to bind straight edges, miter corners, turn sharp curves, and bind scalloped edges, while lying flat along the edge of your quilt.

Start by determining the size of the square or rectangle needed to make enough binding. Lay your fabric on a flat surface with right side up, and mark the four sides as shown (Figure 27). They can be marked with a water erasable pen or by writing on masking tape.

If you are using a square, fold the square in half diagonally and press lightly. Cut along this fold to create two triangles (Figure 28). You now have two bias edges. Place sides A and B right sides together and sew a 1/4" seam using 12-15 stitches per inch. As you sew this seam, overlap the seam allowances so that they cross on the sewing line, approximately 1/4" from the cut edges (Figure 29).

If you are using a rectangle, fold side A down to match side D (Figure 30). Press this diagonal fold lightly and cut along this line to create the bias edges (Figure 31). Place sides A and B right sides together and sew a 1/4" seam using small stitches (Figure 32).

Press this seam open and lay the fabric on a flat surface (Figure 33). Starting at one side that is not marked, draw a parallel line two inches (the binding width) from the bias edge. Continue drawing parallel lines two inches apart on the whole piece of fabric (Figure 34). Be careful not to stretch your fabric as you draw the lines. Trim off the fabric at the end if it is less than 2".

Figure 27

Figure 28

Figure 29

Figure 30

Figure 31

Figure 32

Figure 33

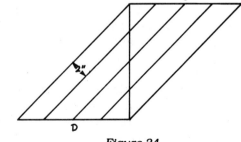

Figure 34

22

Bring sides C and D together to create a tube of fabric (Figure 35). Pin the seam together but first shift one edge of C down so that it matches the first line marked on D (Figure 36). At the other end, the end of D will match the last line on C. This is a strange seam to sew because your fabric will not lie flat. Sew this seam with a 1/4" seam allowance and 12-15 stitches per inch (Figure 37). Press this seam open.

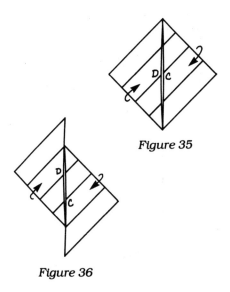

Figure 35

Start cutting at one uneven end along the marked line (Figure 38). When you get to the seam, you will have moved down one line and can continue to cut enough binding for your quilt (Figure 39). To cut binding for a large quilt, place the binding over your ironing board. Keep turning the tube of fabric as you cut the binding.

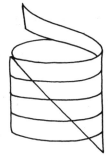

Figure 36

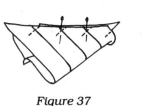

Figure 37

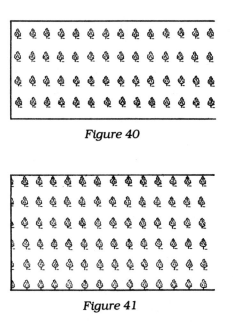

Figure 38

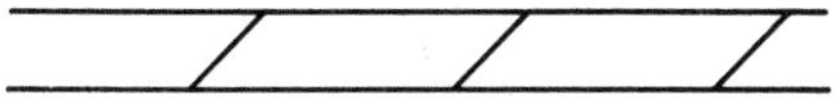

Figure 39

Special Print Binding

Fabrics with small, evenly spaced designs can create very special bindings for your quilt. Designs repeated in straight or diagonal patterns can be cut into straight or bias strips to make unique bindings. A row of small flowers or hearts can be lined up along the edge of your quilt to add the perfect touch.

Figure 40

The method that you use to apply your binding will determine how wide you want to cut your binding strips. The width of one row of designs printed on your fabric will equal the width of your finished binding (and also your seam allowance). Binding applied using the traditional method will have a design on the front and the back of the quilt if there are four designs cut on the width of each strip (Figure 40). French binding will have a design on the front and the back of the quilt if there are six designs on each strip (Figure 41). You may have to adjust your binding width to accommodate enough designs.

Figure 41

Cut strips of fabric to make enough binding for your quilt, each strip having the same rows of designs. The strips can be cut on the straight grain or on the bias depending on the design in the fabric. Some diagonal designs may not be printed on a true bias. Cut the fabric along the design and don't worry about the "true" bias. It is a bias strip and will look beautiful if you apply it carefully. Sew the strips together according to the directions in this chapter, and you will have a very special binding for your quilt.

Figure 42

Figure 43

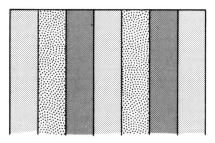

Figure 44

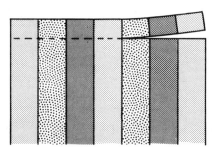

Figure 45

Rainbow Binding

A unique patchwork binding can be made for your quilt by piecing together fabrics from your design. Fabrics and colors can change as patches are repeated around the edge of the quilt. The patches can be the same size as pieces in the quilt, or made from varying sizes. As you finish rainbow binding with hand stitches, choose a thread color that blends with a medium color in your rainbow or matches the back of the quilt.

One method for making rainbow binding is to cut single patches and piece them together to form the binding. Each patch should be cut the width of your binding. The length can repeat a patch size in your quilt or may be cut in random lengths, remembering to add two 1/4" seam allowances to sew the patches together. Sew the patches together with a straight 1/4" seam and press the seams open to distribute the seam fullness (Figure 42). Continue adding patches until you have enough binding length to go around your quilt (Figure 43).

Rainbow binding that repeats the order of the fabrics can be made by sewing strips of fabric together, then cutting the binding strips. Using small machine stitches and pressing the seams open, sew strips of quilt fabric together to make striped yardage (Figure 44). Using a rotary cutter or scissors, cut across the strips at right angles to the seams to make patchwork strips the desired binding width (Figure 45). Sew the binding strips together to make enough binding length to go around your quilt.

Striped Binding

There are several ways to use striped fabric to create special accents for the edge of your quilt.

Binding strips can be cut across the straight grain of the fabric and pieced together. When applied to your quilt, colors and designs from all of the stripes will appear on the binding edge (Figure 46).

Straight strips can also be cut parallel to the striped design (Figure 47). One particular stripe can be positioned to frame the edge of your quilt. Cut your binding strips adding seam allowance to the special stripe that you plan for the front of your quilt.

Binding strips can also be cut on the bias grain of striped fabric. When applied to your quilt, the diagonal stripes will spiral around the edge of your quilt (Figure 48).

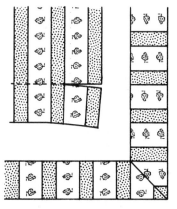

Figure 46

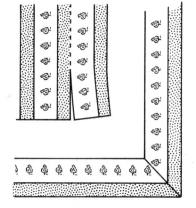

Figure 47

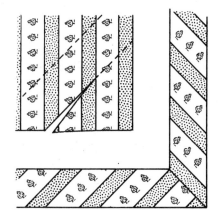

Figure 48

Finishing Your Quilt Without Binding

Left: Quilted corner
Puffy edges
Rounded corner

Below: Wide imitation binding
Appliqued border

25

Finishing Your Quilt With Backing

Right: Overlapped corner
         Mitered corner

Finishing Your Quilt With Binding

Below, clockwise from upper
right: Rounded corner
        Folded mitered corner
        Overlapped corner
        Mitered corner

Finishing Your Quilt With Binding

Above: Corded binding
           Special print binding
           Striped binding cut on the diagonal
           Striped binding cut on the straight grain

Below: Rainbow binding
           Scalloped edges

Finishing Your Quilt With Special Techniques

Above: Pleats
              Covered cording
              Prairie points

Below: Pre-gathered ruffles
              Fabric ruffles
              Eyelet lace

Applying the Binding to Your Quilt

Beginning the Binding

As you begin to sew the binding on to your quilt, take a moment to think about the starting point. Do not start in a corner unless you are planning to overlap the corners or sew the miters. It is easier to fold a miter in a corner than to sew the miter together. If you have rounded off the corner, it is easier to start on a straight edge than on the curve.

Avoid starting to sew the binding in the center of one of the sides of the quilt. Each time that you fold your quilt in half later, it will weaken this spot.

The best place to begin sewing the binding is somewhere between the corner and the center of a side. On a large quilt it may not matter where you start, but on a small wall hanging you will want to choose a starting point that will not show later. The top edge is a good place to begin on a small hanging.

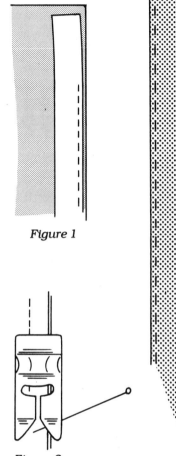

Figure 1

On a large quilt, it is good to start approximately ten inches from a corner. You may want to start sewing at the beginning of a side and sew the binding on to most of the side before you must face sewing the corner curve or miter. Or you might want to sew the first corner right away and save the long edge for last. This depends on your preference. Just remember to avoid starting in the corner or the center.

When you start to sew, do not start right at the beginning of the binding (Figure 1). Instead, leave an unstitched "tail" about two inches long. You do not need to backtack when you begin to attach the binding. This will be stitched as you finish the end of the binding.

Do not pin the binding to the entire quilt before sewing. It's very uncomfortable to sew with all of those pins sticking you. Instead, as you sew, concentrate on the three inches of binding directly in front of the sewing machine needle. Lay these three inches in position and sew. Then go on to the next three inches. Before long those three inches add up to the entire quilt! Be careful not to let your binding stretch as you apply it. Keep the long piece of binding in your lap as you sew, rather than letting it fall to the floor. This will prevent puckers when you are finished. As you sew, if the two layers of binding shift so that the layers are not staying together, use a long straight pin to control the layers in front of the presser foot and needle (Figure 2). This will prevent you from sticking your finger under the needle; the straight pin fits under there much easier.

Figure 2

Before applying the binding by machine, you may want to baste the binding to the edge of the quilt. This will hold the binding precisely in place and prevent stretching when it is stitched on the sewing machine.

Your binding can also be stitched to the edge of the quilt by hand. Use a small running stitch to sew the binding to the three quilt layers (Figure 3). Add a backstitch every two inches to secure your stitches.

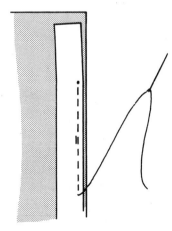

Figure 3

29

Applying the Binding

There are two methods that can be used to apply binding to your quilt. Traditional binding covers the edge of your quilt with a single layer of fabric. Seam allowances are turned under on the front and back of the quilt. A cross section of the quilt (Figure 4) looks like this:

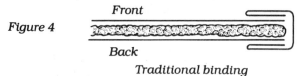

Figure 4

Front

Back

Traditional binding

French binding covers the edge of your quilt with a double layer of fabric. The strip of fabric is folded in half and both seam allowances are sewn to the front of the quilt. The folded edge is then turned to the back to create the binding. A cross section of the quilt (Figure 5) looks like this:

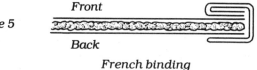

Figure 5

Front

Back

French binding

Traditional Binding

Traditional binding may be cut on the bias or straight grain of the fabric. The strips may be pieced together or cut as a continuous strip. To apply traditional binding that is finished 1/2" on the edge of the quilt, cut strips of fabric that are 2" wide. The length of your binding strip should measure the distance around your quilt plus 9".

To apply traditional binding, press the binding strip in half lengthwise, wrong sides together (Figure 6). Fold each cut edge toward the fold and press again (Figure 7). After basting the quilt edges together, open the folds of the binding and place the binding along the edge of the quilt with right sides together. Match one cut edge of the binding to the cut edge of the quilt (Figure 8). Sew through all layers with a 1/2" seam allowance, using the fold as a guide (Figure 9). After sewing, fold the binding over the edge of the quilt to cover the back (Figure 10). The second fold of the binding should conceal the stitching on the back of the quilt (Figure 11). You may need to trim the quilt edge slightly if the binding will not cover the stitches. Sew the pressed edge of the binding to the back of the quilt by hand, using a blindstitch or slipstitch (Figure 12).

Traditional binding may also be finished completely by machine. Sew the binding strip to the back side of the quilt first. When it is turned to the front of the quilt, it can be stitched by machine along the pressed fold of the binding (Figure 13). For this very quick method of applying binding, refer to "Machine Finished Binding" in the Stitching Guide.

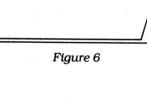

Fold

Figure 6

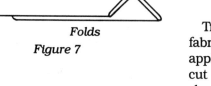

Folds

Figure 7

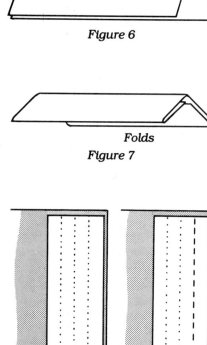

Figure 8   *Figure 9*

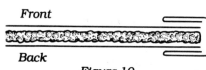

Front

Back

Figure 10

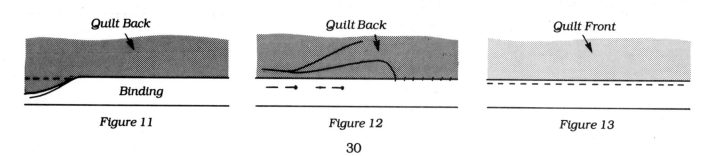

Quilt Back

Binding

Figure 11

Quilt Back

Figure 12

Quilt Front

Figure 13

French Binding

French binding is more durable than traditional binding because it places a double layer of fabric along the edge of the quilt. The double fold also makes it easy to apply a neat and even binding to the edge of your quilt. You can use a light binding on a dark quilt, feeling assured that the dark fabric won't show through the binding.

French binding may be cut on the bias or straight grain of the fabric. The strips may be pieced together or cut as a continuous strip. To make binding that is finished 3/8" on the edge of the quilt, cut strips of fabric that are 2" wide and as long as the distance around your quilt plus 9". This size is easy to handle when sewing and turning it on the quilt. French binding may be cut wider to create wider binding, remembering to account for the double thickness of the fabric.

To apply French binding, first fold the binding strip in half lengthwise. Match the two cut edges, wrong sides together. As you press the binding, let the bottom layer extend slightly (Figure 14). Don't measure this — you just want to be able to see the bottom layer. This will be important when you sew the binding to your quilt. You will be able to see both layers and you will be in control if one shifts or unfolds. Pressing the strip in half with a steam iron also helps the two layers stay together as you sew.

After basting the front, batting, and back of your quilt, match the two cut edges of the binding to the cut edge of the quilt (Figure 15). Sew the binding to the quilt with a 1/4" seam (Figure 16). After sewing, fold the binding over the edge of the quilt to cover the back (Figure 17). The folded edge of the binding should cover the stitching on the back of the quilt. You may need to trim the edge of the quilt slightly if the binding will not cover the seam. Hand stitch the folded edge of the binding to the back of the quilt, using a blindstitch or slipstitch (Figure 18).

French binding may also be finished completely by machine. Sew the binding strip to the back of the quilt first, then turn the folded edge to the front. Sew along the folded edge with the sewing machine (Figure 19). For this very quick method of applying binding, refer to "Machine Finished Binding" in the Stitching Guide.

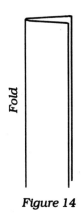

Fold

Figure 14

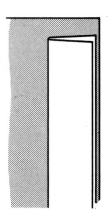

Figure 15

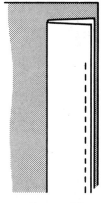

Figure 16

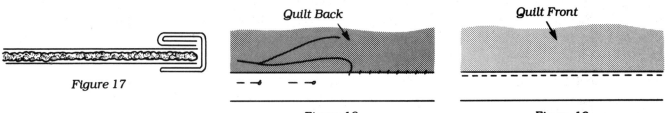

Figure 17

Quilt Back

Figure 18

Quilt Front

Figure 19

Rounded Corners

All quilts have four square corners that need binding, but it may be possible for you to round off the corners on your quilt. This allows you to apply the binding without stopping to miter the corners. Take a good look at the design of your quilt. If there are wide borders on your quilt, or wide areas of background fabric in the corners, you may be able to round off the corners. If there is a very definite square pattern in the corner, it will look better if you miter the corners.

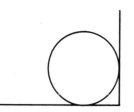

Figure 20

The corners can be rounded easily by using round dishes. The top of a teacup will create a slight curve that looks great on a baby quilt or wall hanging. A saucer will create a more rounded curve for the corners of a quilt, and a dinner plate will round off the corners of a bedspread. Look around and you will find the perfect curve for the corners of your quilt.

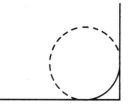

Figure 21

First baste the front, batting, and back of your quilt together. Position your cup or plate in the corner of the quilt so that the circle touches both sides of the quilt (Figure 20). Using a pencil, draw along the curve from side to side, creating a perfectly rounded corner (Figure 21). Repeat this on the other corners of the quilt. Trim off the square corners of the quilt, and baste through the curved layers before you sew the binding on (Figure 22).

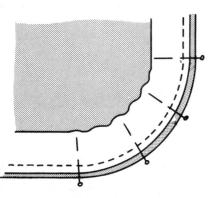

As you apply the binding around the curve at the corner, do not stretch the binding as you place it in position. If the binding is stretched, the corner will not lie flat when it is finished. Position the binding so that the cut edge matches the cut edge of the quilt. Do not clip the binding to get it to go around the curve. As you lay it around the curve, you need to ease the binding fabric so that it matches the quilt on the seam line (Figure 23). It helps to use a long straight pin to ease the binding under the presser foot on your sewing machine. It also helps to take a minute to pin the binding around the curve before you sew. Easing the fabric around the curve will provide adequate fabric to allow the binding to lie flat along the edge when you turn it to the back of the quilt.

Figure 22

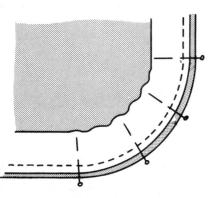

Figure 23

Folded Mitered Corners

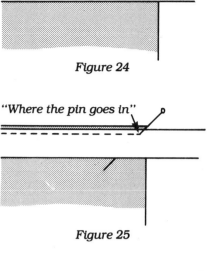

Figure 24

Folded mitered corners have a diagonal fold in the binding that points toward the corner, giving a professional finish to your binding. It only takes a few minutes to fold the miters in the corners, and they provide the perfect accent to many quilts. Small quilts, wall hangings, quilts with thin borders, and quilts with square designs in the corners look especially nice with mitered corners. If you cannot round off the corners of your quilt, then try folded mitered corners. Remember there's only four corners to do. You'll be an expert by the third one!

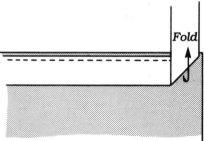

"Where the pin goes in"

Figure 25

Sew your binding along the first edge of the quilt. If you are using French binding, stop stitching 1/4" from the end and backtack (Figure 24). (If you are using traditional binding or if your seam is wider than 1/4", then you will need to stop the width of your finished binding seam.) A straight pin will help you mark the place to stop stitching. Turn your quilt to the wrong side and stick a pin into the corner so that it is 1/4" from each of the edges. Push it straight through all thicknesses (quilt plus binding). The place where the pin comes out on the top marks the place where you will stop stitching. Take another pin and insert it from the front in this spot, using this second pin to hold the binding and quilt together. "Where the pin goes in" signals your place to stop stitching (Figure 25).

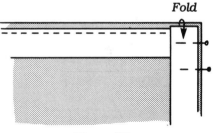

Fold

Figure 26

Fold the binding as shown, so that the binding is folded diagonally and extends straight with the second edge of the quilt (Figure 26). If you fold it back far enough, you can see the last stitch. When you are folding your miter, if there is a binding seam near the fold, ignore it. Do your best to pretend that it's not there and continue. It will be bulky, but it is not a problem. Fold the binding down even with the second edge of the quilt (Figure 27). The fold should be even with the first edge. Use two or three pins to hold this in place. Start sewing the binding 1/4" from the fold, making sure to backtack (Figure 28). This line of stitching continues the line of stitching from the first edge. Again you can stick a pin through the back of the quilt (where the first line of stitching ends) to help mark your starting point (Figure 29).

Fold

Figure 27

Figure 28

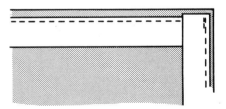

Reverse Side

Figure 29

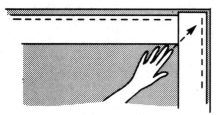

Figure 30

Place your finger under the corner fold and push the fabric toward the point (Figure 30). Fold the binding over the edge and toward the back of the quilt. On the front the fabric automatically folds into a miter (Figure 31). On the back, fold the binding flat over one edge of the quilt (Figure 32). At the end of the side it will form a diagonal fold. As you turn under the second edge, this diagonal fold creates the miter on the back of the quilt (Figure 33). As you fold, look at the back of the quilt and fold the right side first. This will distribute the thickness of the fabric evenly at the point.

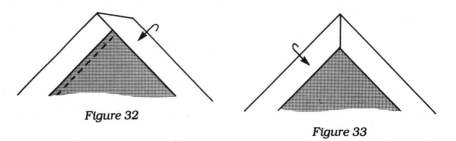

Figure 32

Figure 33

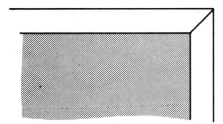

Figure 31

As you hand stitch the binding on the back of the quilt, take three or four blind stitches up the miter fold on the back. Then stick the needle through to the front and take three or four stitches down the miter on the front. Push the needle through to the back of the quilt and continue stitching the binding on to the back of the quilt.

The folded miter method can also be used on angles that are not square (for a six or eight sided quilt, or angles on vests) (Figure 34). As you fold the binding the first time, make sure that the binding strip extends straight with the second edge of the quilt (Figure 35). As you fold it the second time, the fold may not be perfectly even with the first edge because of the different angle (Figure 36). It should still touch the first side at the point, creating a small tuck when you continue stitching the binding.

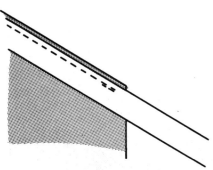

Figure 34

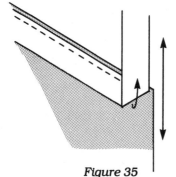

Figure 35

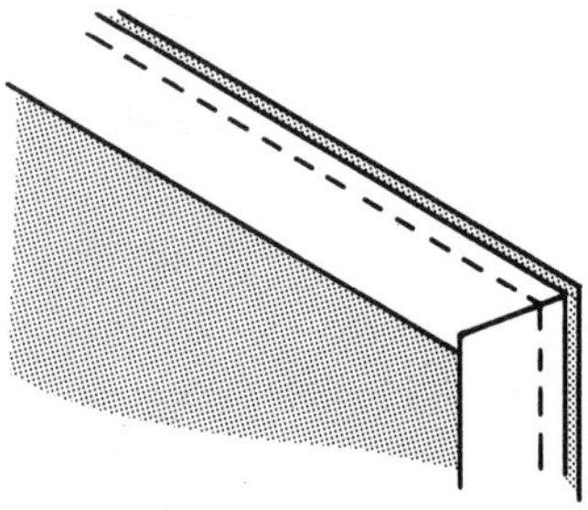

Figure 36

Mitered Corners

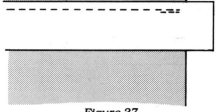

Figure 37

If you do not wish to fold the miters in the corners, you can sew the miters in your binding. To do this, the binding is applied to each side of the quilt separately. Each strip of binding is cut four inches longer than the quilt side. As you place your binding on the edge of the quilt, allow 2" to extend at each end.

Sew the binding on to all four sides of the quilt, stopping 1/4" from the ends (or the width of your binding seam) and back tacking (Figure 37). Fold the binding out from the edge of the quilt, overlapping the two strips at right angles. If you are applying traditional binding, fold the second seam allowance now.

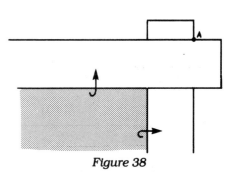

Figure 38

Mark each strip where they cross — point A (Figure 38). On the wrong side of the binding, draw a line from point A into the corner seam — point B (Figure 39). Place your ruler along the stitching line and make a mark at the folded edge of your binding, directly across from the corner seam — point C (Figure 40). Lay your ruler so that it touches point C and the diagonal line. Draw a line from point C to the line — point D (Figure 41).

Place the binding strips right sides together, matching points A together (Figure 42). Sew from B to D to C (Figure 43). Trim the seam to 1/4" and finger press it open. Turn the binding over the edge to the back of the quilt, forming miters on the front and back (Figure 44).

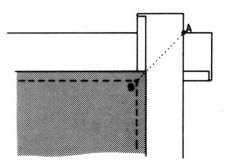

Figure 39

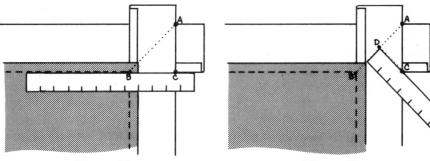

Figure 40

Figure 41

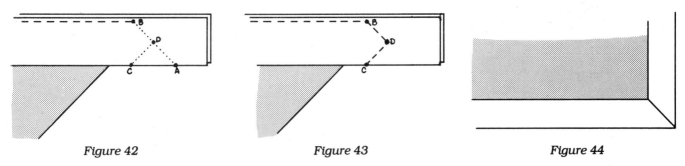

Figure 42

Figure 43

Figure 44

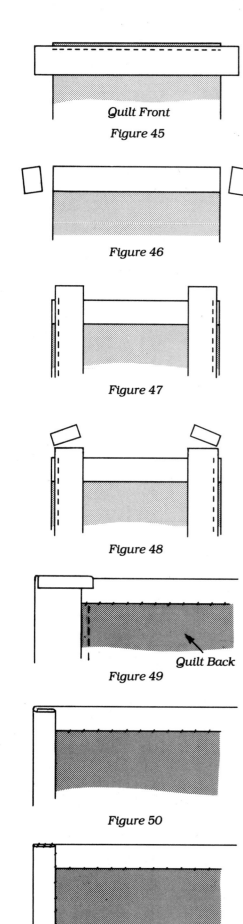

Quilt Front

Figure 45

Figure 46

Figure 47

Figure 48

Quilt Back

Figure 49

Figure 50

Figure 51

Overlapped Corners

If you do not wish to apply the binding in one long piece, the binding can be applied to each side of the quilt separately and overlapped at the corners. Each strip of binding should be cut the length of the quilt side plus four inches. This will allow extra fabric to overlap the binding at the corners.

To overlap the corner pieces, sew the binding to two opposite sides of the quilt, stitching from one cut edge to the other (Figure 45). Fold the binding over the edge and sew the binding to the back of your quilt. Trim off the extra fabric at the ends (Figure 46).

Sew binding on to the other two sides of the quilt, overlapping the first two strips (Figure 47). Trim the ends of the binding, leaving 1/4" on each end (Figure 48). Fold the cut ends of the binding over the first binding strips (Figure 49), then fold the binding to the back of the quilt, enclosing all of the cut edges (Figure 50). Sew the remaining binding to the back of your quilt, stitching the corners with a blindstitch (Figure 51).

Scalloped Edges

Scalloped edges create a beautiful finish, especially on appliqued quilts. Scallops along the edge may reflect part of the pattern, as in some Dresden plate quilts, or you may want to use scallops to accent the style of your quilt. Binding for curved edges should always be cut on the true bias to allow it to stretch around the curves while remaining flat.

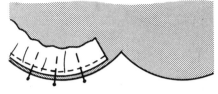

Figure 52

Sewing binding on scalloped edges is a combination of two processes: applying the binding around a curve, and turning an inside corner. If you have rounded off the corners of a quilt to apply binding, then you are half way there!

Of course, the first step is to baste the three layers of the quilt together securely. This is especially important when working with curves, because the bias edges will slide under the presser foot as you sew on the machine. Carefully baste the three layers 1/4" from the curved cut edges. If your scallop curves are marked but have not been cut, you can first apply the binding to the marked fabric and later trim the curves.

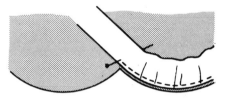

Figure 53

Start to apply the binding on one side of the curve (Figure 52). Starting in the inside corner may cause problems later when you are ending your binding. Starting on the outer edge of the curve may be noticeable when you are finished.

As you position the binding around the curve, do not stretch the binding. Place the binding so that the cut edge of the binding matches the cut edge of the curve. As you pin the binding around the curve, ease the fullness in the binding so that it matches the seam line of the quilt. Pin the binding around one curve at a time before you sew. You should stop sewing at the inside corner (Figure 53). Mark the inside corner point "where the pin goes in" so that you will know where to stop. As you sew around the curve, you can use a long straight pin to help you maneuver the fabric under the presser foot on your sewing machine. This fabric ease will allow the binding to turn over the curve of the scallop and lie flat when it is finished.

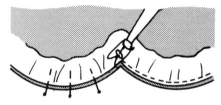

Figure 54

Figure 55

Do not stop and backtack when you get to the inside corner. Leave the needle in the fabric and lift the presser foot. Turn your binding so that it is ready to apply on the next scallop (Figure 54). Pivot the quilt, lower the presser foot, and start stitching on the next scallop for approximately an inch. While the quilt is still under the needle, pin the binding to the next scallop and proceed. There is no need to stop and fold the binding at an inside corner, just pivot and continue sewing.

Figure 56

To turn the binding to the back of the quilt, turn one scallop at a time. When you get to the inside corner, turn one side of the corner to the back and pin it on the back. As you turn the second side of the corner, a tuck will form a folded miter (Figure 55). The deepest part of the tuck will be at the outer edge of the binding. As the binding turns to the back of the quilt, the fold will taper to lie flat along the sewing line (Figure 56). The folded miter may be stitched closed with a blindstitch.

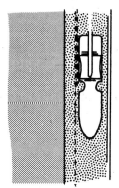

Figure 57

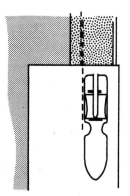

Figure 58

Corded Binding

A very special tailored effect can be added to your quilt by placing a row of covered cording inside the binding.

Make the covered cording following the directions on page 45, covering cording with the desired fabric. The cording should be thin, so that it just adds an accent of color to the edge of your quilt.

Baste the three layers of the quilt together. Sew the cording to the edge of the three layers, using your zipper foot (Figure 57). Use the seam allowance planned for your binding. Then apply the binding on top of the cording, again using your zipper foot (Figure 58). As you turn the binding to the back of the quilt, the cording will appear between the quilt and the binding (Figure 59).

This technique adds a thickness to the edge of the quilt. When planning, you should add 1/4" to the width of your binding so that it will turn over the edge. You may need to trim the edge of the quilt slightly after you apply the binding if it will not fully cover the stitches on the back of the quilt. Before you sew the binding on the back of the quilt, inspect your cording carefully. You may need to re-sew the binding in a few spots to cover the cording stitches.

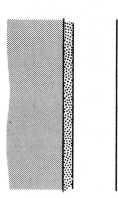

Figure 59

Connecting the Ends of the Binding

When you have stitched the binding to your quilt and returned to the starting place, there is a quick and easy method to end the binding. Stop sewing approximately four inches from the starting point. Cut the end of your binding so that it overlaps the beginning piece one inch (Figure 60). Turn the edge of the end under 1/2" (Figure 61). Insert the beginning "tail" inside the fold of the end piece (Figure 62). Continue to stitch this piece of the binding to your quilt, overlapping the beginning stitches to secure the binding (Figure 63). Fold this portion to the back of the quilt just as you fold the rest of the binding. It may be a little thick in this area, but this is rarely noticed on a large quilt.

To avoid this thickness, there is another method you can use. When you cut the end of the binding, let it overlap the beginning edge two inches. Cut the end diagonally, with the shortest end of the diagonal on top nearest to you (Figure 64). Turn the diagonal edge under 1/4" (Figure 65), and insert the beginning "tail" inside the diagonal fold (Figure 66). Continue sewing the binding on to the quilt (Figure 67). Fold this area to the back of the quilt for a finish that is less bulky. This diagonal seam can be left unstitched, but it is usually hand stitched when the binding is attached to the back of the quilt.

If you want to sew a real seam at this point, cut the beginning and end so that they overlap 1/2" (Figure 68). Unfold the ends and place them right sides together. Sew them together with a 1/4" straight seam (Figure 69). Press the seam open to distribute the thickness as you finish sewing the binding (Figure 70).

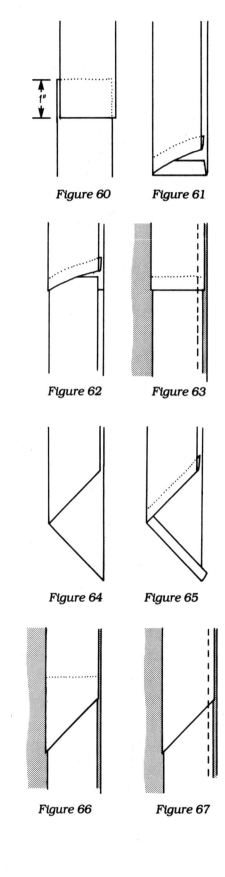

Figure 60   *Figure 61*

Figure 62   *Figure 63*

Figure 64   *Figure 65*

Figure 66   *Figure 67*

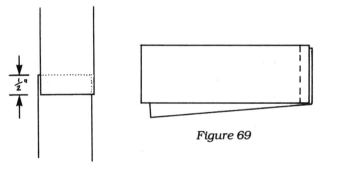

Figure 68

Figure 69

Figure 70

Finishing Your Quilt With Special Techniques

There are several special finishing techniques that are fun to add to your quilts. Prairie points, pre-gathered lace, ruffles, pleats, and covered cording all create special effects as they frame the edge of your quilt.

If your quilt has already been quilted, these finishing touches are first stitched to the front of the quilt and the batting. Move the backing out of the way as you sew. Attach the prairie points, lace, ruffles, pleats, or cording to the right side of the front of the quilt using a 1/4" seam allowance and stitching through the batting. These trims are sewn all around the edge of the front (Figure 1). After the trim has been stitched on, trim the batting close to the seam. Fold the trim out away from the quilt, turning the seam allowance in toward the quilt (Figure 2). Turn the seam allowance of the backing fabric under 1/4" and pin the back of the quilt to the back side of the trim, covering the seam and the machine stitches (Figure 3). Complete the back of the quilt using a blindstitch or slipstitch (Figure 4).

If you are sewing the trim to your quilt before you quilt or tie it, first sew the trim around the front edge of the quilt only. Then place the front and back of the quilt right sides together, sandwiching the trim inside. Sew a 1/4" seam around the edge of the quilt, sewing with the front on top and leaving an opening to turn the quilt right side out later. Attach the batting, referring to the machine finishing directions in "Finishing Your Quilt Without Binding" on page 9 to complete your quilt.

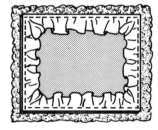

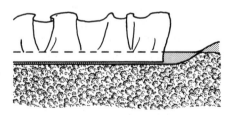

Figure 2

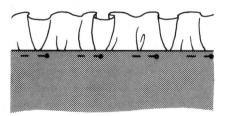

Figure 1

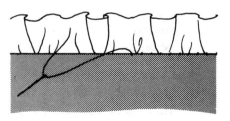

Figure 3

Figure 4

Prairie Points

Prairie points are small folded triangles placed along the edge of the quilt. They may repeat a triangular motif in the design of your quilt, duplicate the color scheme of the quilt, or accent the design. The prairie points may all be the same color, or they may repeat the fabrics in the quilt.

To make one prairie point, start with a three inch square of fabric. Fold the square in half diagonally, wrong sides together (Figure 5). Then fold it diagonally again, forming a smaller triangle (Figure 6). The longest edge of the triangle will be attached to the edge of the quilt. Make another prairie point, then slip the fold of one point into the opening of the other (Figure 7). This is how they fit together to go around your quilt. They may overlap a little or a lot, depending on the look you want or on the amount of fabric you have available.

Every 20" of quilt edge takes approximately twelve points when they are overlapped. It will take approximately a yard and a half of fabric to make enough points for a large quilt.

For a large quilt, it is possible to make a long string of points before sewing them on to the quilt edge. Start feeding the first point into your sewing machine, placing the cut edges on the right as you sew, and the folded tip under the needle (Figure 8). Sew for an inch with a basting stitch, then feed the next point into the first one, overlapping approximately 3/4" (Figure 9). Continue sewing and feeding points until you have enough length for the edges of your quilt. Make a separate string of points for each side of your quilt.

If your quilt is small, or if you want to be more accurate about the placement of the points, you may want to position the points on the edge of the quilt before you sew them together. Start by placing one point in the center of one side of your quilt, having the long cut edge of the triangle matching the cut edge of the front of your quilt (Figure 10). Position a point at each end of the side, making sure that the folded edges of the triangles aim in the same direction as the first one (Figure 11). Place another point between these triangles, then continue to arrange more triangles in between until the side of the quilt is full (Figure 12). Put each triangle inside the other to make a continuous line of prairie points. They may overlap a little or a lot, just make sure that they are evenly spaced.

In the corners of the quilt, place two triangles as shown so that they fit together side by side (Figure 13). They should not overlap. When you sew them on to the quilt edge, pivot your seam where they meet. When they are turned to point out, there will be a perfect corner (Figure 14).

To sew the prairie points on to your quilt, first pin the cut edge of the points to the cut edge of the front of the quilt. If you have made a long string of points, make sure that you have the same number of points on opposite sides of your quilt. You may need to shift a few end points to fit the side of the quilt accurately. Sew around all four edges of your quilt front with a 1/4" seam to attach the points. To finish sewing your quilt together, refer to the directions on page 40.

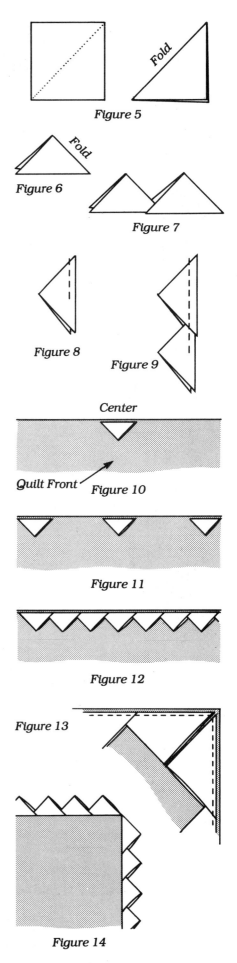

Figure 5

Figure 6

Figure 7

Figure 8

Figure 9

Center

Quilt Front

Figure 10

Figure 11

Figure 12

Figure 13

Figure 14

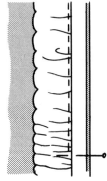

Figure 15   Figure 16

Pre-Gathered Ruffles and Lace

Ruffles and gathered lace can be added to a quilt for a special effect. Ruffles can be purchased as pre-gathered yardage or you can make your own to coordinate with the fabrics and colors in your quilt.

If you are purchasing pre-gathered lace or ruffling, you need the distance around the quilt plus a quarter of a yard.

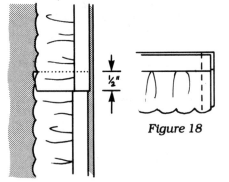

Figure 18

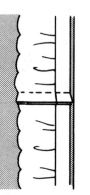

Figure 17

To sew pre-gathered lace or ruffling to your quilt, place it right sides together on the edge of the front of the quilt, matching the cut edge of the quilt and the binding on the edge of the ruffle. Do not sew the first two inches of the ruffle, leaving a "tail" for finishing later. Use a 1/4" seam, sewing along the inside edge of the ruffle gathers to include the ruffle binding within the seam (Figure 15). Sew straight along one edge of the quilt, stopping one inch from the corner. For this last inch as you approach the square corner, use a long straight pin to push the ruffle under the presser foot, adding more fullness to the gathers (Figure 16). When you get to the corner, leave the needle in the fabric, lift the presser foot, and pivot to stitch the next side. Continue adding fullness to the gathers for another inch. This will give your ruffle enough fullness to "fan out" around the corner when it is turned right side out. If your corners are rounded off, it is still helpful to add some fullness as you sew the ruffle or lace around the curve.

When you stitch around the entire quilt and get to the place where you started, there are several ways to finish the ruffle. To make a seam in the ruffle, cut the two ends so that they overlap 1/2" (Figure 17). Put the two ends right sides together and sew a 1/4" seam (Figure 18). Lay this continuous piece on the edge of the quilt and continue stitching it to the quilt (Figure 19).

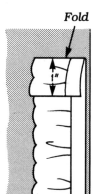

Fold

Figure 19   Figure 20

For a quicker finish, you can fold the "beginning tail" back one inch (Figure 20). Cut the "finishing tail" so that it overlaps the first one by one inch (Figure 21). Just sew over these folds and your ruffle is complete with no raw edges showing on the front. The fullness of the ruffles will hide the cut edges.

If your pre-gathered ruffle is doubled, you can conceal the cut edges by cutting the tails so that they overlap 2". Fold back the raw edges of one side 1/2" and slip the other tail inside. This will provide a finished edge on the front and the back (Figure 22).

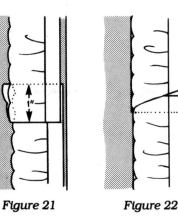

Figure 21   Figure 22

Sew around all four edges of your quilt to attach the ruffles or lace. To finish sewing your quilt together, refer to the directions at the beginning of this chapter on page 40.

Making Your Own Ruffles

Fabric ruffles can be cut on the bias or straight grain of the fabric. The width of the cut fabric should be twice the width of the finished ruffle plus seam allowances. For example, if you want a two inch finished ruffle, cut a 4 1/2" strip of fabric. (2" for the front, 2" for the back, and two 1/4" seam allowances.) This makes a ruffle that will be pretty on the front and back of the quilt, and avoids sewing a long hem on the edge of the ruffle. The length of the ruffle should be at least twice the distance around your quilt. If a 36" square baby quilt measures 4 yards around the edges, you need to cut 8 yards of fabric strips for the ruffle.

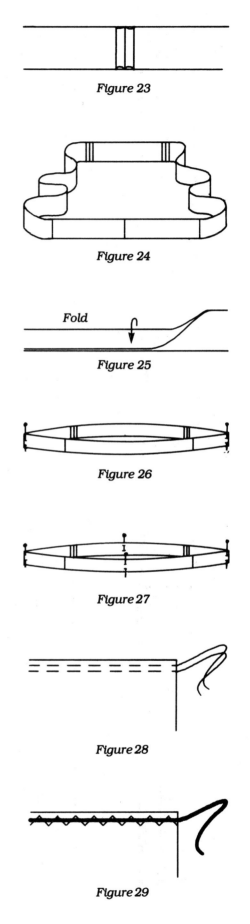

Figure 23

Figure 24

Figure 25

Figure 26

Figure 27

Figure 28

Figure 29

To make the ruffle, first stitch the fabric strips together to make one long ruffle. They can easily be sewn together with straight 1/4" seams, placing right sides together. Press the seams open to distribute the thickness of the seam (Figure 23). Sew a seam at the end to make the strip into one long continuous loop (Figure 24).

Fold the ruffle in half, wrong sides together, so that the cut edges match (Figure 25). Press the fold with a steam iron to help the fabrics stay together. Fold the length to divide it in half, and mark these points with pins (Figure 26). Fold each half in half again to divide it into quarters, and mark these points with pins (Figure 27). It helps to gather each quarter separately. These marks can also be used to position the ruffle evenly on the quilt.

To gather the ruffle, you can use the method of sewing two parallel lines of machine stitches, 1/8" and 3/8" from the cut edges of the ruffle (Figure 28). Sew with the longest stitch available on your machine, loosening the tension if possible. Gather the ruffle by pulling the bobbin threads (and praying that they don't break!)

There is another method that is very helpful for gathering long ruffles. Set your sewing machine for the longest, widest zigzag stitch that it will make. Lay a piece of heavy thread or crochet cotton 1/8" from the cut edges of the ruffle. Zigzag over this thread, being careful not to stitch into it (Figure 29). When you are finished, this thread can be pulled easily to gather the ruffle.

Gather the ruffle until it fits the edge of your quilt. The four pins placed along the ruffle can be matched to the centers of the sides of the quilt. For a square quilt, fold each quarter in half to find the corner points. For a rectangular quilt, allow twice as much ruffle for each side length. For a large quilt, you may want to divide the length again to make it easier to handle. Distribute the fullness evenly along the edge, but add extra gathers one inch on each side of the corners to allow the ruffle to lie flat when it is turned out.

Sew around all four edges to attach the ruffle to your quilt front with a 1/4" seam allowance. To finish sewing your quilt together, refer to the directions at the beginning of this chapter on page 40.

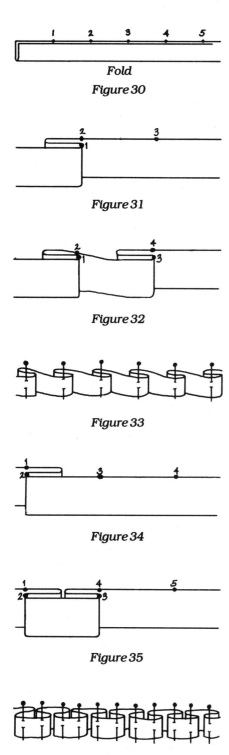

Fold

Figure 30

Figure 31

Figure 32

Figure 33

Figure 34

Figure 35

Figure 36

Pleats

Fabric pleats along the edge of your quilt are made using a folded strip of fabric similar to the ruffle. The pleated strip should be cut on the straight grain of the fabric. The length of the strip should be twice the distance around your quilt for knife pleats, three times the distance for box pleats. The width of the strip should be twice the width of the desired pleats plus seam allowances. If you want pleats that are 1-1/2" wide, cut a strip that is 3-1/2" wide (1-1/2" for the front, 1-1/2" for the back, and two 1/4" seam allowances).

As you consider using pleats along the edge of your quilt, remember that pleats are easy to apply if the square corners of your quilt have been rounded off. Refer to "Rounded Corners" on page 32 to prepare the corners of your quilt. Ease extra fullness into the pleats so that they lie flat around the curve.

Piece together a strip long enough to make the pleats and fold the strip in half lengthwise (refer to "Making Your Own Ruffles" for complete directions). Using a pencil or water erasable marker, make marks one inch apart along the cut edge of the strip (Figure 30). This will make pleats that are one inch wide. For smaller pleats, make the marks 1/2" or 3/4" apart.

To make knife pleats all folded in the same direction, fold mark number one forward to match mark number two, creating a pleat (Figure 31). Then fold mark number three to mark number four (Figure 32). Continue folding every other mark until you have pleated the entire strip (Figure 33). These pleats can be pinned or machine basted before they are applied to your quilt.

To make box pleats, fold mark number two back to match mark number one (Figure 34). Then fold mark number three forward to match mark number four, making a box pleat (Figure 35). Continue folding one pleat back, then one pleat forward, until the entire strip is pleated (Figure 36).

Pleats are applied to the front of the quilt with a 1/4" seam. To finish sewing your quilt together, refer to the directions at the beginning of the chapter on page 40.

Covered Cording

Covered cording creates a thin line of trim along the edge of your quilt without adding binding. It is inserted between the front and back of the quilt to accent a color or fabric in the quilt. It gives the illusion of very thin binding.

You will need cording, available in most fabric stores, the length of your quilt edges plus 1/4 yard. This cording may be thick or thin, according to the look you desire. To cover the cording, you will need fabric strips cut one inch wide and the length of your cording. They may be cut on the bias or on the straight grain, and can be cut continuously or pieced in strips. If you are applying cording to curves, it will be easier to handle if cut on the bias.

To cover the cording, fold the fabric strip in half lengthwise, wrong sides together. Insert the cording, pushing it inside the fold (Figure 37). Using a zipper foot on your sewing machine with the needle set in the left notch on the foot, sew the two cut edges of the fabric together, enclosing the cording (Figure 38). The foot should ride comfortably next to the cording on the left side. The stitches should be long basting stitches, 6 stitches per inch. When you have enclosed the entire piece of cording, trim the seam allowance evenly to 1/4" (Figure 39).

Covered cording is applied to the front of the quilt. Lay the cording along the edge of the quilt so that the cut edge of the cording and the cut edge of the quilt meet. Still using the zipper foot, sew the cording to the quilt using a 1/4" seam allowance (Figure 40).

If you are sewing cording around a curve, avoid stretching it as you sew around. It does not have to be eased like binding, just sew it evenly to the edge of the quilt. You may need to clip the cording seam allowance a few times to keep it lying flat (Figure 41). Do not clip any further than the stitching line. If you are sewing a corner, stop sewing one inch from the corner. Clip the cording seam allowance three or four times near the corner. Continue stitching to the corner. Stop with the needle in the fabric and lift the presser foot. Turn the fabric slightly and take two stitches (Figure 42). Lift the presser foot again and turn the fabric to sew the next side. These two stitches will help the corner look good when it is turned to the right side.

When you get around to the starting point, cut the cording so that the two tails overlap one inch. Open the stitches on the end tail and cut off one inch of the inside cording (Figure 43). Turn the cut edge of the end under 1/4", either straight or diagonally (Figure 44). Insert the beginning, covering all raw edges (Figure 45). Match this to the edge of the quilt, and continue the seam (Figure 46).

When you sew the front and back of the quilt together by machine, continue to use a zipper foot. It will ride easily next to the cording thickness and position your stitches correctly. If you sew with the front of the quilt on top, you will be able to see your previous stitches. Sew to the left of these stitches to hide them in the seam of the finished quilt. To finish sewing your quilt together, refer to the directions at the beginning of this chapter on page 40.

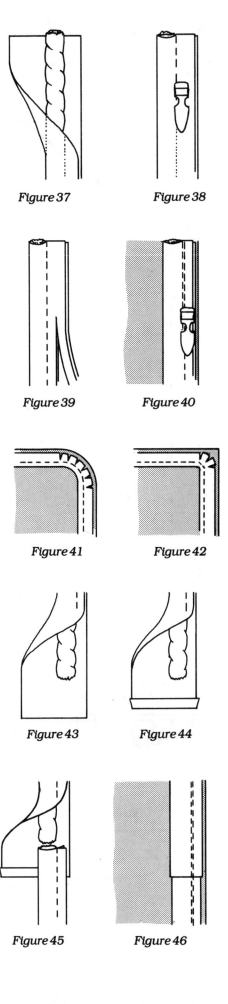

Figure 37   Figure 38

Figure 39   Figure 40

Figure 41   Figure 42

Figure 43   Figure 44

Figure 45   Figure 46

Stitching Guide

Hand Stitches

If you do not wish to use the sewing machine, you can use hand stitches to sew the front and back of the quilt together, to sew binding strips together, to make covered cording, or to sew the binding to your quilt.

A running stitch is used to sew layers of fabric together. Use a single strand of thread about 18" long and tie a knot in one end. Use a quilting needle, or a longer one if you prefer. Take two or three short running stitches at a time, sewing in and out through the layers of fabric to attach them together. Every two inches make a small backstitch to strengthen the running stitches (Figure 1). End your stitches by sewing two small backstitches, bringing the needle through the loop to secure your thread.

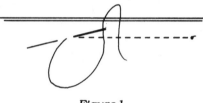

Figure 1

Quilting Stitches

Quilting stitches are short running stitches used to sew the front, batting, and back of your quilt together. To begin quilting, tie a single knot in the end of an 18" length of quilting thread. Start to quilt by inserting the needle through the top layer of the quilt about 3/4" from the point where you want to start stitching. Slide the needle through the batting layer and bring the needle out at the starting point. Gently tug on the thread until the knot pops through the fabric and is buried in the batting. Take a backstitch and begin quilting, making a small running stitch that goes through all three layers. Take two, three, or four stitches at a time, trying to keep them straight and even.

When you end your quilting stitches, make a single knot approximately 1/4" from your quilt top. Take one more backstitch into your quilt, tugging the knot into the batting layer, and bringing the needle out 3/4" away from your stitches. Clip the thread and let the end disappear into your quilt (Figure 2).

Basting Stitches

Basting stitches are used to hold layers of fabric together while you sew the final seam. They are usually removed after the seam has been sewn. Basting stitches are long running stitches, stitched with the "ins" and "outs" approximately one inch apart. They are usually stitched one or two stitches at a time. You do not need to make backstitches because these stitches should be easy to remove later (Figure 3).

Hand Quilting Stitch

Figure 2

Basting Stitches

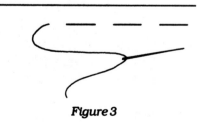

Figure 3

Finishing Stitches

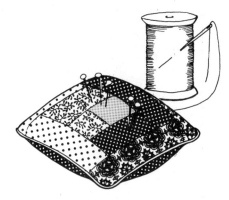

These stitches are used as you finish the front and back of the quilt without binding, after turning the back of the quilt to finish the front of the quilt, or after applying binding or special finishings. The stitches that are used are the blindstitch, sometimes called the applique stitch, and the slipstitch, sometimes called the ladder stitch. These stitches are invisible when your quilt is finished.

Use a quilting needle, or a longer one if you prefer. Start with a single strand of thread approximately 18" long and tie a knot in one end. If you use a double thread, the threads tend to twist around each other and eventually weaken the stitches. If your binding is a different color than your quilt, the thread should match the binding. It should match the front of the quilt when sewing the front and back together. It should match the back when finishing prairie points, ruffles, pleats, lace, and covered cording.

As you finish your quilt, do not pin the binding around the entire quilt. It's fun to use four or five pins, pinning a few inches at a time as you sew by hand. Before long, those pins will travel around the whole quilt. As a special bonus, the quilt will not stick you if you curl up in it to complete your last stitches.

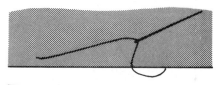

Figure 4

Blindstitch or Applique Stitch

A blindstitch is appropriate to use on all areas of the binding. It is used when you make your own binding or when you use the quilt backing to finish the edges. This stitch may also be used to sew the back of the quilt to prairie points, ruffles, pleats, or cording. The blindstitch is a good stitch to use on folded mitered corners or at the end of the binding. It is traditionally used to sew appliques to background fabric.

Start by bringing your needle up through the edge of the binding, as close as possible to the folded edge (Figure 4). Make a very small stitch by "jumping" straight off the edge of the binding and into the quilt (Figure 5). This stitch should be taken just past the machine stitches that were used to apply the binding to the quilt. When the binding is finished, these machine stitches will be covered. Slide your needle under the top layer of the quilt, travelling through the batting for approximately 1/8" to 1/4". These stitches should not go all the way through to the other side of the quilt. Bring the needle back up through the quilt and the folded edge of the binding, picking up only one or two threads from the fold (Figure 6). Continue to repeat this process, pulling the thread slightly after every four or five stitches (Figure 7). The stitches should disappear into the seam.

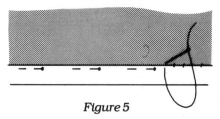

Figure 5

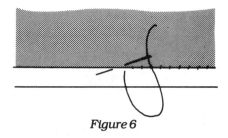

Figure 6

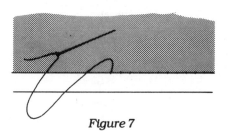

Figure 7

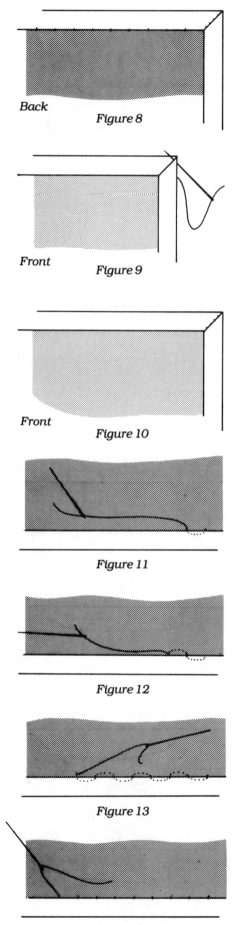

Back

Figure 8

Front

Figure 9

Front

Figure 10

Figure 11

Figure 12

Figure 13

Figure 14

When you get to a folded mitered corner, you will feel more secure if you stitch the miter folds closed. Pin the miter folds so that they are neat, using the needle or a long straight pin to tuck the folds in place evenly. Stitch up the miter on the back side of the quilt using four or five blindstitches (Figure 8). At the point, move the needle through to the front of the miter (Figure 9) and stitch the miter on the front of the quilt, continuing to the inner miter corner (Figure 10). At this time, check to see if there is a space between the rows of machine stitches in the corner. One or two small stitches can close this easily. Now stick the needle through to the back side of the quilt and continue to attach the binding on the back side. This same process can be used to close the fold where you begin and end your binding.

Slipstitch or Ladder Stitch

A slipstitch is used to finish the front and back without binding, to sew the straight edges of the binding, and to attach the back of the quilt to prairie points, ruffles, pleats, and cording. It is a good stitch to use on long straight areas.

Start by bringing your needle up through the folded edge of the binding. Take a small stitch in the fold of the binding, approximately 1/8" to 1/4" long (Figure 11). Move straight across to the quilt and take a small stitch in the top layer of the quilt, just past the machine stitches that were used to apply the binding (Figure 12). Now move your needle straight across to the binding and take a small stitch in the fold. Repeat until you have five or six stitches between the quilt and the binding. The stitches will resemble the rungs on a ladder (Figure 13). Pull lightly on the thread until the stitches disappear, sewing the binding and quilt together (Figure 14).

Ending Your Thread

When you start to run out of thread, lift up the binding and take a small stitch into this area. Take two backstitches to tie a knot in the thread, stitching through the loops as you take the stitches (Figure 15). These will be under the binding when you continue, and will never be seen again. When you get to the end of the binding, take two small back stitches near the last stitch, then slide the needle through the top layer of the quilt about an inch and bring the thread out (Figure 16). Clip the thread and you are done!

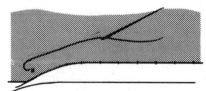

Figure 15

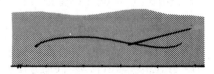

Figure 16

48

Machine Stitches

When you are constructing your quilt, sewing the front and back together, or applying binding or special finishings, set the stitch length on your machine to 10 - 12 stitches per inch. This size stitch is very secure, but is also just the right size for your seam ripper (just in case you need to use it!)

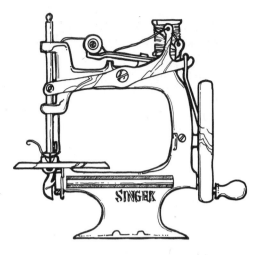

When machine-piecing your quilt, sewing binding strips together to make a long strip, or making continuous cut binding, set the stitch length on your machine to a shorter 12 - 15 stitches per inch. These small stitches will hold the pieces together without backtacking, especially as you cut continuous binding strips apart.

Use a machine basting stitch with a length of 6 stitches per inch when you are basting quilt layers together, preparing a string of prairie points, gathering ruffles, basting folds in pleats, or making covered cording. These longer stitches hold fabric together but are easy to remove if necessary.

Machine Finished Binding

It is possible to apply the binding on your quilt entirely by using the sewing machine. To apply traditional or French binding, the first step is to sew the binding to the back of the quilt, rather than the front. When the binding is turned to the front of the quilt, the finishing machine stitches will be on the front.

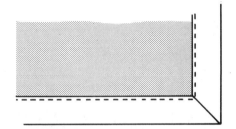

Figure 17

Turn the binding to the front of the quilt. Carefully pin all around the quilt to keep the binding in place and prevent it from slipping. Pin the mitered corners securely. Make sure that the binding covers the machine stitches that were used to sew the binding to the quilt.

Machine stitch the binding to the quilt along the fold at the inner edge of the binding (Figure 17). You will be sewing through the binding fold, the three layers of the quilt, and the binding on the back of the quilt. This may be very bulky, but it can be controlled. You may need to use a long straight pin to adjust the fold as it goes under the machine presser foot. The machine stitches produce a nice edge to the binding on the front of the quilt, but it's difficult to control the position of the stitches on the back of the quilt. This may not be the method to use on your heirloom or prize-winning quilt, but it is a quick way to sew the binding on.

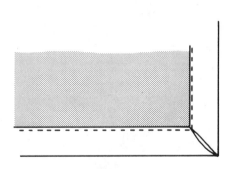

Figure 18

If your quilt has mitered corners, it is best to ignore the miters as you sew around the binding by machine. Turn the corner when you get to the inside miter corner and continue stitching (Figure 18). The miter will survive if you just leave it folded, but you may want to close the miter using blind stitches.

As you stitch around the quilt, continue sewing over the point where the binding starts and ends (Figure 19). Like the miters, this area may remain folded or can be hand stitched.

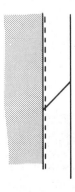

As you finish sewing the binding with your sewing machine, overlap your beginning stitches for two inches and backtack.

Figure 19

Sharing Your Happy Ending

You've finished your quilt by sewing the last three inches of binding securely, and you can't wait to take it upstairs and fling it on the bed to admire it's total beauty! But wait! Take a few moments to share some information with the future. Sign your newest work of heart with your name and other information you would like to remember. Record the date, celebrate the occasion, and dedicate it to someone special. Your quilt is now a part of history and you want to remember its story. Don't you wish your grandmother had done this with her quilts?

There are several ways to sign your quilt. You can use a thin-line permanent marker to write the information in a corner on the back of the quilt. You can write with a pencil or water-erasable pen, then embroider or quilt your inscription. You can also type on fabric or embroider a separate "designer" label to sew to the back of your quilt.

This information will bring back special memories after you have finished ten more quilts. Your family and friends will cherish your special "signed" gifts. It will help historians of the future remember you, and help assure a Happy Ending for your quilt.

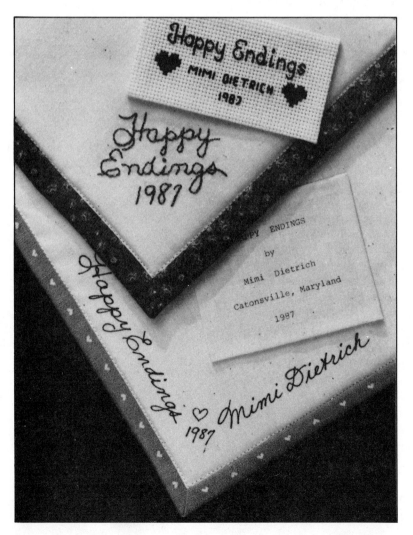

Finishing Clothing and Home Accessories

The techniques throughout this book may be used on projects other than flat quilts. Quilted clothing such as vests, jackets, skirts, and even petticoats need finished edges. Vests are three dimensional quilts, needing binding around the edges and armholes. Clothing may also be finished by using the lining to cover the edge, or completed without extra binding. Sometimes ruffles, lace, pleats, covered cording, or prairie points are inserted between the garment and the lining, just as they are attached on the quilt edge.

Most quilters wouldn't be caught without at least one tote bag. A special quilt block can be finished off and used as a pocket. Binding can be applied to two separate blocks and they can be stitched together to form a tote. The top of the bag can be completed and strengthened with the use of binding.

Craft items and home accessories may also require finished edges like the quilts in this book. Small wall quilts and doll quilts are treated just like full size quilts. Pillows can be constructed using these techniques to sew the front and back together. Ruffles, lace, pleats, covered cording, and prairie points can be added to pillows in the same way that they are applied to quilts. Covers for small kitchen appliances, sewing machines, and computers need binding around the bottom edge.

Let your imagination discover other ways to use the finishing techniques and you can create your own special Happy Ending!

new and bestselling titles from

America's Best-Loved Craft & Hobby Books™

America's Best-Loved Quilt Books®

NEW RELEASES
All Through the Woods
American Quilt Classics
Amish Wall Quilts
Animal Kingdom CD-ROM
Batik Beauties
The Casual Quilter
Fantasy Floral Quilts
Fast Fusible Quilts
Friendship Blocks
From the Heart
Log Cabin Fever
Machine-Stitched Cathedral Stars
Magical Hexagons
Potting Shed Patchwork
Repliqué Quilts

APPLIQUÉ
Artful Album Quilts
Artful Appliqué
Colonial Appliqué
Red and Green: An Appliqué Tradition
Rose Sampler Supreme

BABY QUILTS
Easy Paper-Pieced Baby Quilts
Even More Quilts for Baby: Easy as ABC
More Quilts for Baby: Easy as ABC
Play Quilts
The Quilted Nursery
Quilts for Baby: Easy as ABC

HOLIDAY QUILTS
Christmas at That Patchwork Place
Holiday Collage Quilts
Paper Piece a Merry Christmas
A Snowman's Family Album Quilt
Welcome to the North Pole

LEARNING TO QUILT
Basic Quiltmaking Techniques for:
    Borders and Bindings
    Divided Circles
    Hand Appliqué
    Machine Appliqué
    Strip Piecing
The Joy of Quilting
The Simple Joys of Quilting
Your First Quilt Book (or it should be!)

PAPER PIECING
50 Fabulous Paper-Pieced Stars
For the Birds
Paper Piece a Flower Garden
Paper-Pieced Bed Quilts
Paper-Pieced Curves
A Quilter's Ark
Show Me How to Paper Piece

ROTARY CUTTING
101 Fabulous Rotary-Cut Quilts
365 Quilt Blocks a Year Perpetual Calendar
Around the Block Again
Biblical Blocks
Creating Quilts with Simple Shapes
Flannel Quilts
More Fat Quarter Quilts
More Quick Watercolor Quilts
Razzle Dazzle Quilts

SCRAP QUILTS
Nickel Quilts
Scrap Frenzy
Scrappy Duos
Spectacular Scraps

CRAFTS
The Art of Stenciling
Baby Dolls and Their Clothes
Creating with Paint
Creepy Crafty Halloween
The Decorated Kitchen
The Decorated Porch
A Handcrafted Christmas
Painted Chairs
Sassy Cats

KNITTING & CROCHET
Clever Knits
Crochet for Babies and Toddlers
Crocheted Sweaters
Fair Isle Sweaters Simplified
Irresistible Knits
Knit It Your Way
Knitted Shawls, Stoles, and Scarves
Knitting with Novelty Yarns
Paintbox Knits
Simply Beautiful Sweaters
Simply Beautiful Sweaters for Men
The Ultimate Knitter's Guide

Our books are available at bookstores and your favorite craft, fabric and yarn retailers. If you don't see the title you're looking for, visit us at www.martingale-pub.com or contact us at:

1-800-426-3126

International: 1-425-483-3313

Fax: 1-425-486-7596

E-mail: info@martingale-pub.com

For more information and a full list of our titles, visit our Web site or call for a free catalog.